WATER

Paola Jervis

Illustrated by
Lorenzo Cecchi, Lorenzo Orlandi,
Alessandro Rabatti, Daniela Sarcina

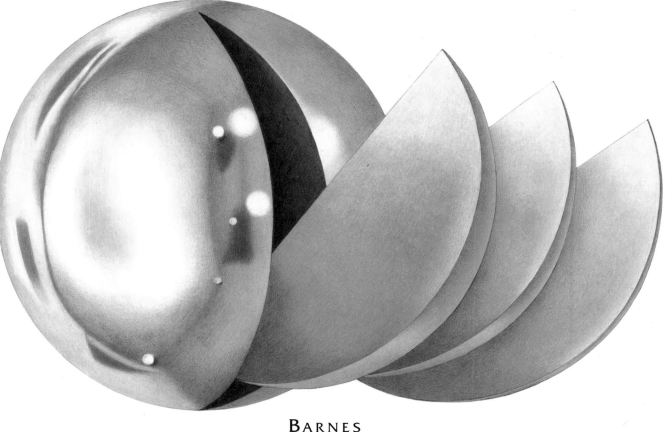

BARNES
& NOBLE
BOOKS
NEW YORK

DoGi

Produced by
Donati Giudici Associati,
Florence
Original title:
La risorsa acqua
Text:
Paola Jervis
Illustrations:
Boni-Galante Studio
(Simone Boni, Lorenzo
Cecchi, L.R. Galante),
Carlo Ferrantini,
Lorenzo Orlandi,
Tiziano Perotto,
Francesco Petracchi,
Alessandro Rabatti,
Claudia Saraceni,
Daniela Sarcina, Donato
Spedaliere
Computer graphics:
Bernardo Mannucci
Design:
Francesco Lo Bello,
Laura Davis
English translation:
Simon Knight
Editor, English edition:
Ruth Nason
Typesetting:
Ken Alston –
A.J. Latham Ltd

© 1995 Donati Giudici
Associati s.r.l.
Florence, Italy
First English-language
edition © 1996
Watts Books

First American edition
© 1997
Barnes & Noble, Inc.
This edition published by
Barnes & Noble, Inc. by
arrangement with DoGi srl

ISBN
0 7607-0597-6

HOW TO USE THIS BOOK

THE MAIN TEXT
On each double
page, the text
under the main
title gives an
overview of the
topic covered.

ILLUSTRATIONS
The main
illustrations focus on
the importance of
water in different
aspects of our lives
from earliest times to
the present day.

**FURTHER
INFORMATION**
Smaller drawings
and photographs
introduce scientific
principles,
examples and
important people
connected with the
topic under study.

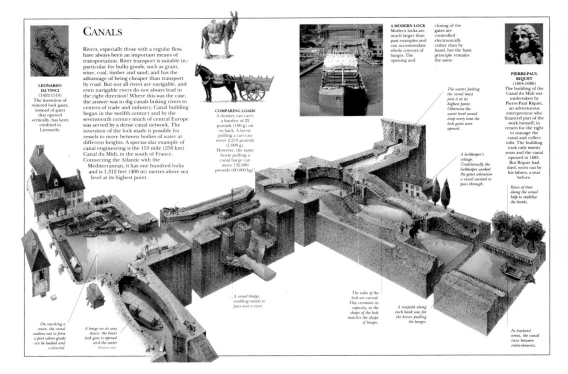

CANALS

LEONARDO DA VINCI (1452-1519)
The invention of mitered lock gates, instead of gates that opened vertically, has been credited to Leonardo.

Rivers, especially those with a regular flow, have always been an important means of transportation. River transport is suitable in particular for bulky goods, such as grain, wine, coal, timber and sand, and has the advantage of being cheaper than transport by road. But not all rivers are navigable, and even navigable rivers do not always lead in the right direction! Where this was the case, the answer was to dig canals linking rivers to centers of trade and industry. Canal building began in the twelfth century and by the seventeenth century much of central Europe was served by a dense canal network. The invention of the lock made it possible for vessels to move between bodies of water at different heights. A spectacular example of canal engineering is the 155 mile (250 km) Canal du Midi, in the south of France. Connecting the Atlantic with the Mediterranean, it has one hundred locks and is 1,312 feet (400 m) metres above sea level at its highest point.

COMPARING LOADS
A donkey can carry a burden of 22 pounds (100 g) on its back. A horse pulling a cart can move 2,210 pounds (1,000 g). However, the same horse pulling a canal barge can move 132,600 pounds (60,000 kg)!

A MODERN LOCK
Modern locks are much larger than past examples and can accommodate whole convoys of barges. The opening and closing of the gates are controlled electronically rather than by hand, but the basic principle remains the same.

PIERRE-PAUL RIQUET (1604-1680)
The building of the Canal du Midi was undertaken by Pierre-Paul Riquet, an adventurous entrepreneur who financed part of the work himself, in return for the right to manage the canal and collect tolls. The building took only twenty years and the canal opened in 1681. But Riquet had died, worn out by his labors, a year before.

The waters feeding the canal must join it at its highest point. Otherwise the water level would drop every time the lock gates were opened.

A lockkeeper's cottage. Traditionally the lockkeeper worked the gates whenever a vessel wanted to pass through.

Rows of trees along the canal help to stabilize the banks.

On reaching a town, the canal widens out to form a port where goods can be loaded and unloaded.

A barge on its way down: the lower lock gate is opened and the water drains out.

A canal bridge, enabling vessels to pass over a river.

The sides of the lock are curved. This increases its capacity, as the shape of the lock matches the shape of barges.

A towpath along each bank was for the horses pulling the barges.

In lowland areas, the canal runs between embankments.

**HISTORICAL
BACKGROUND**
Each topic is set in
a historical
context, to show
the reasons for and
consequences of
new developments.

**IMPORTANT
PEOPLE**
Information is
provided about
people who have
contributed to
research and
development.

CREDITS

The original and previously unpublished illustrations in this book may be reproduced only with the prior permission of Donati Giudici Associati, who hold the copyright.

Abbreviations: t, top; b, bottom; c, center; l, left; r, right.
ILLUSTRATIONS: Simone Boni, 32–33c; Lorenzo Cecchi, 16–17c, 26–27, 44bl, 44tr, 44c; Carlo Ferrantini, 29tr, 34–35, 36tl, 39r; L.R. Galante, 37cl; Lorenzo Orlandi, 6–7c, 10–11, 12–13, 14–15, 18–19, 20–21, 24–25, 40–41, 42–43; Tiziano Perotto, 36b, 37bl, 38–39c; Francesco Petracchi, 32tr, 39r; Alessandro Rabatti, 22–23c; Andrea Ricciardi, 16cl, 35tr; Claudia Saraceni, 25tr, 28–29c, 36cl; Daniela

Sarcina, 6tl, 6cl, 7t, 7cr, 7bl, 8–9, 23tl, 23cr, 30–31, 36tr, 37tl, 37tr, 37br, 45t; Donato Spedaliere, 16tr, 38bl, 44–45bc.
Cover: Alessandro Rabatti.
Title page: Daniela Sarcina.

PHOTOGRAPHS: A.G.E./Granata Stock Photo, 19tr; © Curzio Baraggi/Grazia Neri, 40tc, 40tr; © W. Cody/West Light/Granata Stock Photo, 9cr; DoGi Archive, 13br, 17br, 25tr, 25cl, 25cr, 25br, 29tl, 32tl, 33tr; Paolo Donati, 22tl; © Brian Drake/Viesti Associates/Granata Stock Photo, 18tl; © Walter Fiorani/Granata Stock Photo, 19tc; Simon Fraser/Science Photo Library/Grazia Neri, 41tr; © Lowell Georgia/Photo Researchers/Grazia Neri 41br; Granata Stock Photo, 14tr; © Frank

Grant/International Stock/Granata Stock Photo, 33tl; IFA/Granata Stock Photo, 4bc, 6bc, 8tr, 9tl, 11tr, 12tl; L'Illustration/Grazia Neri, 34tr; © Michael Lewis/Viesti Associates/ Granata Stock Photo, 18cl, 43br; © Ronn Maratea/International Stock/Granata Stock Photo, 19tl; NASA/Science Photo Library/ Grazia Neri, 20tr; © J.A. Pavlovsky/ Sygma/Grazia Neri, 20cr; Scala-Firenze, 25bl; Superstock/ Granata Stock Photo, 11tl.

DoGi s.r.l. have made every effort to contact copyright holders. If any omissions have been made, this will be corrected at reprint.

CONTENTS

LIFE DEPENDS ON FRESH WATER

The entire biological balance of the Earth depends on the water that covers three quarters of the planet's surface. Life also depends on water – but only a minute proportion of the Earth's vast supply is in a form that is useful for humans. This is the fresh water that forms rivers and lakes, collects underground and bubbles up in the form of springs. It is this water that we use every day, and which is taken up by the roots of plants, which are at the base of all food chains. People through history first learned to use this water for irrigation, then channeled it to their growing cities, and managed to tame and use it as a source of energy. Until the beginning of the twentieth century, it was thought that supplies of fresh water were endless and indestructible, even though they were unequally distributed across the planet. Now things have changed. With the spiralling growth of world population, and pollution from industry and agriculture, we are realizing that water is not only a limited and increasingly expensive resource, but also frighteningly easy to harm and lose. One of the burning issues of world politics in the coming decades will be how to manage water resources more carefully than in the past.

WATER USE IN POOR COUNTRIES
In villages in some African countries, people have to fetch their water from wells and carry it by hand. Here the amount of water used per person per day may be as little as 5-10 quarts.

WATER USE IN RICH COUNTRIES
In cities in the United States and Europe, the average amount of water used by one person per day is about 130 gallons (500 l). Of this, about 40 percent is flushed down toilets and 37 percent is used for washing purposes.

ORIGINS
It is thought that, when the planet Earth was formed, it was surrounded by a dense cloud of gases. These eventually condensed to give water.

SOURCE OF LIFE
Plants are at the base of all food chains, as they make their own food by photosynthesis – a process that uses sunlight, carbon dioxide, chlorophyll in the leaves and water. The water, with minerals from the soil dissolved in it, is absorbed through the roots.

A RENEWABLE RESOURCE
The Earth's fresh water is constantly recycled, as water evaporates from the surface of the planet and returns to it again as rain or snow.

FRESH WATER
Life depends on fresh water. Only 1.1 percent of all the Earth's water is fresh water in a form that is actually available to us.

UNEQUAL SHARES
Over 600 million people live in the world's arid areas where annual rainfall is less than 12 in (300 mm). Here the normal amount of water available per person per year is under 260 gal (1,000 l). In a country like Canada, the figure is 26,000 gal (100,000 l).

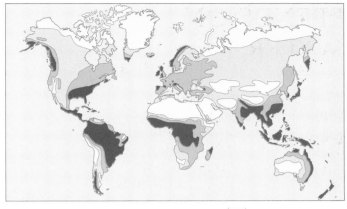

0-1 in
10-20 in
20-40 in
more than 40 in

ARID LANDS
Some deserts have had no rain for over five years.

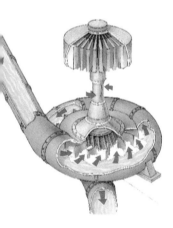

TURBINE
The power of water can be used to generate electricity. Today, 6 percent of the world's electrical energy is produced in hydroelectric power stations.

ENERGY
For centuries, the water wheel was the main source of power not supplied by domestic animals.

STEAM
Water is essential for running a steam engine. This new type of machine revolutionized industrial production in nineteenth-century Europe.

70%
60%
50%
40%
30%
20%
10%
0

Agricultural uses
Industrial uses
Domestic uses
Waste

USING WATER
In 1990, according to a United Nations estimate, 65 percent of fresh water resources were used in agriculture; 24 percent by industry; and 7 percent for domestic purposes. 4 percent was being lost or wasted.

POLLUTION
Pollution is one of the causes of water shortage, simply because dirty water is unusable. The discharge of domestic and industrial wastes has poisoned rivers and made it impossible to use many wells and springs.

5

VENUS
The planet Venus is permanently shrouded in cloud. Scientists believe that the planet was formed, at first, in the same way as the Earth. However, because Venus is closer to the Sun and rotates on its axis more slowly, the temperature there has remained extremely high—more than 878°F (470°C)—and so the clouds of vapor have never condensed.

Scientists studying the planet Earth think that, when it was formed, five thousand million years ago, the quantity of water that is around today already existed – but in the form of vapor released during the formation of the planet's crust. At that time, the Earth was surrounded by a dense atmosphere, rich in gases and electricity but poor in oxygen. It experienced constant volcanic eruptions and enormous movements of molten rock. Hundreds of millions of years later, as the Earth's surface gradually cooled, the water vapor began to condense. This led to hundreds of years of torrential rain, which speeded up the cooling process and profoundly altered the environment. The first rivers were formed, and also enormous reservoirs of water which eventually flowed together to become the oceans. It is thought that life developed in the warm ocean waters.

THE HYDROSPHERE
Earth has been called the blue planet. Seen from space, it appears as a globe almost completely covered in water, with dry land emerging here and there and a generous amount of cloud cover. All the water that is present on the Earth, whether it is in liquid, solid or gaseous form, is known as the hydrosphere (from the Greek for "water").

VOLCANOES
As when the Earth was new, volcanoes today release water vapor into the atmosphere. But unlike in the beginning, only a small part of this vapor comes from original water deep inside the Earth. Most is from water that has filtered down through the rock and been reheated.

THE FIRST FORMS OF LIFE

Scientists think that life began with single-celled organisms that appeared in water one thousand million years after the formation of the Earth. Two thousand million years later, multi-celled organisms appeared, and a thousand million years after that, marine vertebrates evolved. Eventually, living organisms emerged from the oceans to adapt to life on land.

HYDROGEN AND OXYGEN

Every water molecule consists of two atoms of hydrogen and one of oxygen: a structure represented by the chemical formula H_2O. Water is normally found in the liquid state, but can also exist as a solid or a gas. When heated to 212°F (100°C), it turns to water vapor (steam). (It also evaporates at lower temperatures, but more slowly.) When cooled to below 32°F (0°C), water becomes solid, turning into ice. At the same time, it increases in volume.

THE ORIGIN OF LIFE

In 1953, Stanley L. Miller, a biochemist at the University of Chicago, tried to reproduce in the laboratory the conditions that were thought to have prevailed on Earth millions of years ago. The experiment was based on the hypothesis that life began in the oceans as a result of the interaction of gases in the atmosphere and ultraviolet light from the Sun. To prove this, Miller enclosed a mixture of water, hydrogen, ammonia and methane in a glass ball and subjected it to ultraviolet radiation. A few days later, he found that amino acids and other organic compounds had formed in the mixture: the building bricks of living matter!

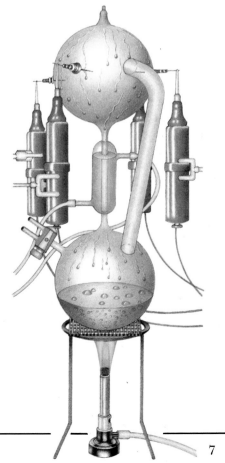

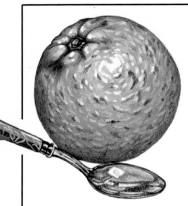

HOW MUCH WATER IS AVAILABLE?

Water covers three quarters of the Earth, but the percentage of it that we can actually use is very small indeed. We need fresh water. Ninety-seven percent of the Earth's water is, however, the salt water of seas and oceans. The remaining 3 percent is fresh water, but the greater part of this is locked up in the polar icecaps or deep inside the Earth, where it is difficult to tap. The water we can actually draw on – from springs, rivers, lakes, aquifers and the atmosphere – amounts to approximately 119,000 cubic miles (500,000 cu km), only about one three-thousandths of the total volume.

COMPARISONS
The volume of all the water found on Earth, compared with the total volume of the planet, is like the volume of water that can be held in a teaspoon, compared with the volume of an orange. Some teaspoon, though! We are talking about 333,200,000 cubic miles (1,400,000,000 cu km) of water!

OCEANS AND SEAS
323,680 cubic miles (1,360,000 cu km) Sea water contains, by weight, about 3.5 percent dissolved salts. The salt content may vary, depending on the rate of evaporation and the amount of fresh water discharged into the sea by rivers.

ICE AGES
The amount of the Earth's water locked up as ice has varied with time. Since the Earth was formed, there have been several Ice Ages, periods during which a thick layer of ice covered much of the now-temperate zones. These periods have alternated with times of milder conditions, when the icefields melted and the water level of the oceans rose.

Oceans and seas.

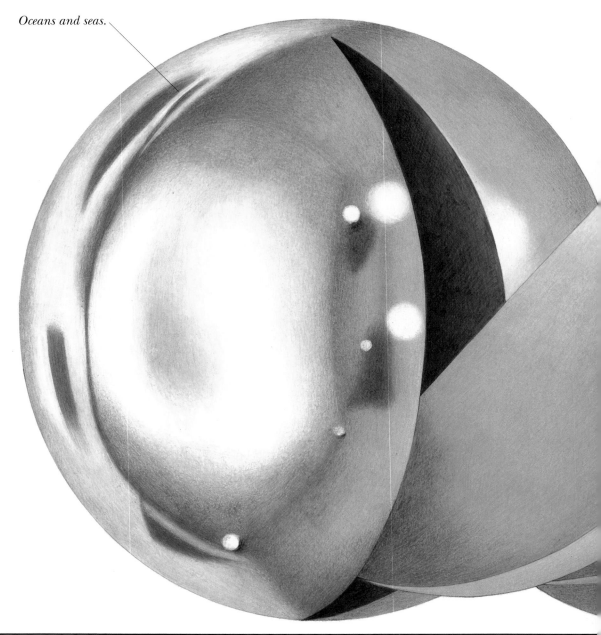

POLAR ICECAPS
7,140,000 cubic miles (30,000,000 cu km) The polar icecaps represent more than three quarters of the planet's reserves of fresh water.

UNDERGROUND WATER
1,904,000-2,142,000 cubic miles (8,000,000-9,000,000 cu km) Deposits of ground water laid down in the geological past are renewed only over very long periods. Deeper deposits are often salty.

AVAILABLE FRESH WATER
119,000 cubic miles (500,000 cu km) This figure includes the water that is held in the atmosphere, as a result of evaporation, and which will later fall as rain or snow.

Polar icecaps.

Underground water.

RESERVOIR
To give yourself some idea of what 119,000 cubic miles (500,000 cu km) of water would look like, imagine a reservoir the size of Spain and 3,280 feet (1,000 m deep).

Fresh water available for use.

THE WATER CYCLE

The fresh water available for us to use is limited in amount, but it is constantly being recycled. Every year, thanks to the heat of the Sun, some 119,000 cubic miles (500,000 cu km) of water are evaporated from the Earth's surface and transferred to the atmosphere, forming clouds. Sooner or later, the water vapor in the atmosphere condenses and falls back to Earth as precipitation, such as rain, snow or hail. Most of the water that is evaporated comes from the oceans; just a small proportion evaporates from the land. In fact, more water falls on land than is evaporated from its surface. This is because part of the water evaporated from the oceans, driven by winds and air currents, precipitates onto land. The excess of precipitation over evaporation accounts for runoff, the complex phenomenon whereby water is returned to the oceans by rivers and groundwater outflows. This exchange balances the whole cycle, and ensures that living organisms receive the water they need.

The water that falls on land consists of water taken up from the land's surface by evapotranspiration and also some 10 percent of the water evaporated from the oceans, which accounts for approximately 5,950 cubic miles (25,000 cu km) per year.

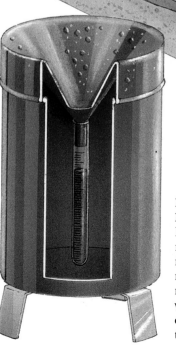

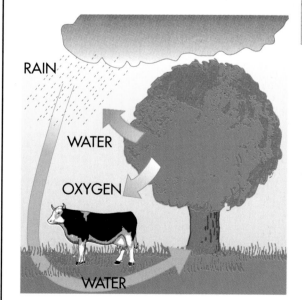

EVAPOTRANSPIRATION

Water is transferred from land to the atmosphere by both evaporation and transpiration – known together as evapotranspiration. Transpiration is the release of water vapor from the leaves of plants.

MEASURING RAINFALL

Rainfall is measured with a rain gauge. The rainfall in different regions of the world occurs in different patterns through the year, expressed in millimeters of rain per month. Knowing rainfall patterns makes it possible to predict water availability and prepare for droughts and floods.

CLOUDS

Clouds hold water in the form of vapor and suspended water droplets. Driven by the wind, they transport water from one part of the planet to another. This is how some of the water evaporated from the oceans precipitates on land.

THE SUN

The Sun provides the force for the water cycle, as it warms the Earth and causes evaporation. Stretches of water heat up more slowly than areas of land, but also hold their heat longer. Differences in temperature between areas of water and areas of land give rise to hot and cold air currents, and it is these which drive clouds and cause rainfall.

As water from the oceans evaporates into the atmosphere, it is purified of its salt content. This is a never-ending process.

Some of the water which falls on land does not evaporate but runs off to the oceans.

90 percent of the water evaporated from the oceans returns directly to its source.

WATER FOR LIFE

Water is a major part of all living matter. It plays an essential role in almost every process that occurs in plants and animals. All organisms, including plants, absorb the substances they need for growth dissolved in water. Weight for weight, plants need more water than animals do. In fact, 90 percent of the water plants absorb through their roots is released into the atmosphere in the form of water vapor. Plants use water, together with sunlight and the carbon dioxide in the air, to convert mineral substances into organic matter. In animals, water plays an essential part in all vital processes. In particular, it serves to regulate their internal chemistry and maintain a constant fluid balance.

AN ESSENTIAL ELEMENT
Almost all the chemical substances in the Earth's crust are soluble in water. It is normally dissolved in water that these substances are transmitted to the living organisms that need them. Together with the oxygen in the air, water plays a part in most chemical reactions.

PHOTOSYNTHESIS
Plant roots absorb water from the soil. It rises to the leaves, in which a substance called chlorophyll enables sunlight to break down the water into hydrogen and oxygen. The hydrogen, combined with carbon dioxide from the air, makes sugar and starch – food for the plant. Most of the oxygen passes into the air. Photosynthesis is essential to all life, as plants are at the base of all food chains.

1. The roots absorb a solution of water and mineral salts from the soil.

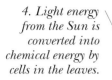

4. Light energy from the Sun is converted into chemical energy by cells in the leaves.

CELLS
All living material is made of cells. Each cell has a nucleus surrounded by the cytoplasm – a material that is mostly water and in which float special organisms called organelles. Water accounts for 65-90 percent of a cell's weight.

6. The phloem sap is channeled back down the stem to every one of the plant's cells.

5. The xylem sap is converted into a nutritious juice (phloem sap) by photosynthesis.

3. The xylem sap reaches the leaves of the plant.

2. The solution, known as xylem sap, is forced up the stem of the plant.

7. The phloem sap reaches the roots.

AQUATIC CREATURES
Some animals, for instance, jellyfish, consist almost entirely of water. Others, such as sponges, feed by filtering gallons of sea water through their bodies every day.

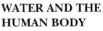

THE CIRCULATORY SYSTEM OF PLANTS
Water containing mineral salts from the soil (xylem sap) is absorbed by the roots and channeled upwards to the leaves. It is converted by photosynthesis into a juice (phloem sap) rich in carbohydrates, for redistribution to all the plant's cells, including those in the roots.

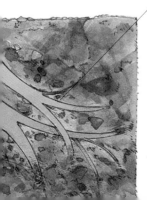

WATER AND THE HUMAN BODY
In a male human being, water accounts for 70 percent of total body weight; for a woman, the proportion is 60 percent. Each day we need to take in between 2 and 3 quarts of water in our food and drink. Our internal fluid balance is maintained by the emission of water vapor from the lungs, the evacuation of feces and urine, and perspiration through the skin.

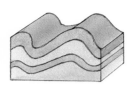

SHAPING THE LANDSCAPE

SERIES OF FOLDS
Movements of the Earth's crust caused colossal upheavals and warped the various layers of rock, resulting in series of folds. Over millions of years, the action of water has eroded these folds, transforming them into the mountains and valleys that we know today.

The Earth's great mountainous areas formed as a result of both volcanic activity and upheavals of the sea bed caused by movements of the planet's crust. However, the particular landscapes with which we are familiar, consisting of mountains, valleys, hills, rivers and lakes, are the work, above all, of water. Over millions of years, water has shaped our environment, as it has eroded rock and carried the eroded material elsewhere. Every river basin is an example of this continuing process. Rain falling violently begins to wear away rock. Then the water that is not absorbed by the ground runs over the surface, cutting itself a course from high to low land that, in time, becomes a valley. Streams on both sides of the valley run into the river below. Materials eroded by the water are transported by the river as it follows its course down towards the coast, and eventually they are deposited on flat land or in the sea.

THE GRAND CANYON
More than 5,248 ft (1,600 m) deep, the gorges cut by the Colorado river in Arizona are thought to be the result of erosion continuing over 10 million years.

Tributary.

Meanders.

A delta forms when the river deposits material at its mouth and the tide and the movement of the sea's waves are not strong enough to carry it away.

As it nears the sea, the river slows down and deposits almost all the sediment it is carrying. Its course becomes less well defined and curves called meanders form.

RAIN
A large drop of rain can strike the ground at a speed of about 22 mph (35 km/h). When rain hits rock, it breaks off tiny pieces which are carried away by the river water and deposited further downstream.

Glacier.

Lake.

Fed by many streams and torrents, the mountain section of a river is steep and swells rapidly after rain. In this section, features caused by erosion are noticeable.

In the section of the river between mountain and plain, both erosion and sedimentation take place. The water carves out a wide-V-shaped channel.

FLOODS
The example of a funnel helps us understand why floods occur. The funnel overflows when water is poured into it too quickly, or when its mouth is too narrow or partially obstructed.

DRAINAGE BASIN
A drainage basin is an area of land from which all rainwater eventually runs into the same single watercourse. It is something like a huge funnel, gathering rainwater from a vast area and directing it into one channel. A line of high ground separating two drainage basins is called a watershed.

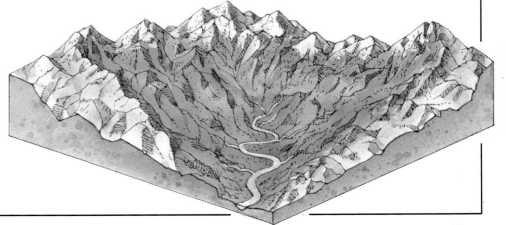

LIVING WITH WATER

Like all animals, humans need water to live and so, from earliest times, they made their homes near water sources, such as springs, rivers, ponds or lakes. In the early Stone Age, people hunting animals for food ventured far from home and needed to carry a small water supply with them. The first water containers were made, often from animal skins. However, it was obviously best to live near water. Water was not only useful for drinking. Fish and crustaceans could be taken from it, to eat. Plants grew abundantly in the fertile soil near the water's edge and these were another source of food. Reeds and brushwood could also be used for building shelters. The presence of water in an area attracted people to stay and by the later part of the Stone Age the first permanent human settlements were established near rivers and lakes. Humans soon learned to travel over water, first sitting astride tree trunks and then making and using proper boats.

THE CAMEL
Some mammals have a system for storing water, which enables them to survive for several weeks without drinking. The camel is probably the best-known example. Humans are not equipped in this way. They can survive for barely four days without water.

SHELTERS
To protect themselves from the weather, people first made their homes in caves and then, in the later part of the Stone Age, began to build huts. Some of these were made from mammoth bones and animal skins.

A palisade protected the settlement from wild animals and other enemies.

In areas that were sometimes marshy, roads were often made of pieces of tree trunks covered with a thick layer of brushwood.

CONTAINERS
Hands hold water just long enough for you to drink it; but they cannot carry water. The oldest known containers for water were made from animal skins stitched together. Their shape was copied when clay containers were first made.

The framework of this hut consisted of thick stakes driven into the ground. The walls were made of interwoven branches daubed with a mixture of clay and straw.

The ditches dug around the huts to extract clay were then used for dumping trash. By studying their contents, archeologists have been able to deduce the diet and many of the habits of the people who lived there.

Before man learned to build bridges, it was not possible to cross large rivers. Travel had to follow the tops of the highest land. It made travelling longer, but avoided rivers and marshy lowlands.

The pitched roof, thatched with straw or reeds, projected at both sides to protect the walls of the hut from the rain.

It may be that people first crossed rivers sitting astride a tree trunk. Later, the tree trunk was dug out to make room for baggage: the first boat?

WOODEN PILES

In the nineteenth century, archeologists found the remains of prehistoric huts built on wooden piles, in the beds of lakes. This made them think that the huts had been built over water. Later it was realized that the huts had been built on the banks of the lakes, whose level had risen, flooding the surrounding area.

THE ORIGINS OF AGRICULTURE

Plants of high food value, such as grains, grew spontaneously in many areas after rain or, on river banks, after annual flooding. Hunter-gatherers of the Mesolithic period (the middle part of the Stone Age), some 10,000 years ago, became aware of this and made regular visits to such areas when the grain ripened. However, it was a very long time before people began deliberately to plant seed in the mud, in the expectation that it would germinate and grow. Perhaps bumper crops persuaded them to settle down and devote themselves primarily to farming. They learned to select seed from the fullest, least fragile ears, to turn over the soil with a spade to assist germination, and to increase the area of fertile land by building irrigation channels and retaining walls. Farmed in this way, the land could support larger groups of people, and so communities were able to settle permanently in one place, near their crops.

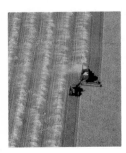

DEPENDING ON RAIN
When farmers rely exclusively on rain to water their crops, the harvest they achieve in any year obviously depends on the amount and regularity of rainfall that year. As the weather is not constant, harvests tend to vary considerably from one year to the next.

EARLY TOOLS
Archeologists have found small stone sickles, mortars and grindstones at early Stone Age sites. These prove that grains were harvested from the wild long before they were cultivated. The spade and, from c.3500 BC, the plow are linked to settled farming.

GAINING BY IRRIGATION
Crops watered by rainfall alone produce one pound (.45 kg) of food for every 118 gallons (448 l) of water they receive. On irrigated land, productivity is double that. Nowadays, one sixth of the world's agricultural land is irrigated, and it produces roughly one third of the world's food.

WHEAT
Ten thousand years ago, people living in the region described as the Fertile Crescent began to cultivate the grain-bearing plants that grew there spontaneously. (Today this region includes Israel, Syria and Iraq.) Repeated selection has produced the grain wheat and barley.

RICE
Rice is another of the world's major grains. Like wheat, it was also harvested long ago from the wild. From 5000 BC, it was cultivated in the valleys of southern China. Irrigation and selection have improved the yield. It is now possible to obtain two rice crops a year.

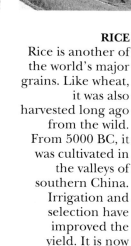

CORN
The origins of corn are less well known than those of wheat and rice. However, it is certain that corn was being cultivated in the Tehuacan region of Mexico six thousand years ago. At first, it bore only a small ear, not the fat cob with which we are familiar today.

THE START OF IRRIGATION
Irrigation techniques were first employed in 5500 BC, in Mesopotamia, at points where rivers descended to the plain. People built simple dams across the branches of a river in order to divert the water into ditches, and it was then conveyed along these to the surrounding land. This consisted of alluvial mud from the river itself.

Egypt, Gift of the Nile

The Egyptians devised one of the most perfect systems of irrigated agriculture of ancient times. They lived in an arid region, with virtually no rainfall, but they made brilliant use of the regular floods of the river Nile, which were caused by monsoon rainfall far away on the highlands of Eastern Africa. By persistent hard work over more than a thousand years, the Egyptians transformed the Nile valley into one of the most fertile areas of the Mediterranean. They achieved this by building dams and canals, embankments and complex systems for raising water. Their ability to control the Nile's waters, organize labor and increase agricultural production gave rise to one of the world's great civilizations. Its prosperity was greatly admired by the Greek historian Herodotus, who lived in the fifth century BC. He described Egypt as the "gift of the Nile."

THE ASWAN DAM
Egypt today no longer relies on the annual Nile flood. Water is now distributed where it is needed, all the year round, from Lake Nasser, an enormous reservoir that was formed by constructing the Aswan Dam. As a substitute for the fertile Nile mud, chemical fertilizers now have to be applied to the land. However, the advantages of the dam outweigh the bad points. It produces hydroelectricity for the whole of Egypt.

In July, when the flood began, the water of the Nile overflowed its banks and spread over the farmland.

SHADDUF
A *shadduf* is a simple mechanical aid for lifting water from a canal to the land where it is needed. Using a multiple *shadduf* system, it is possible to raise water 33 ft (10 m) or more.

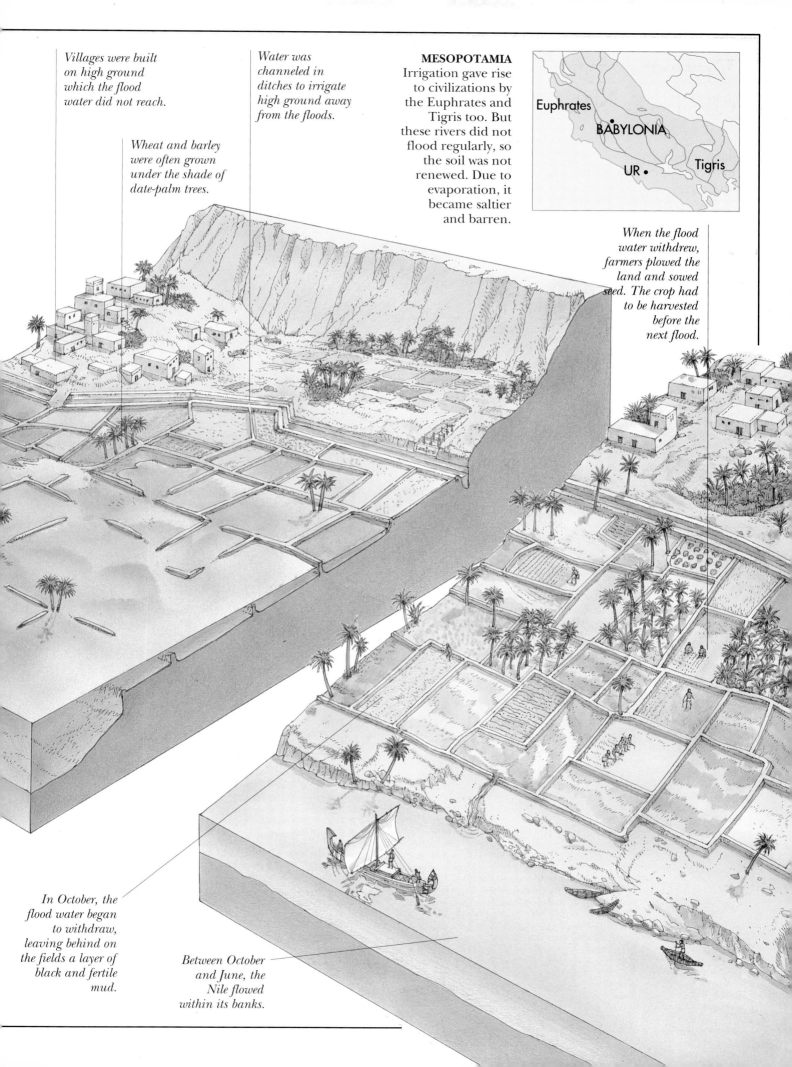

Villages were built on high ground which the flood water did not reach.

Water was channeled in ditches to irrigate high ground away from the floods.

Wheat and barley were often grown under the shade of date-palm trees.

MESOPOTAMIA
Irrigation gave rise to civilizations by the Euphrates and Tigris too. But these rivers did not flood regularly, so the soil was not renewed. Due to evaporation, it became saltier and barren.

Euphrates

BABYLONIA

UR •

Tigris

When the flood water withdrew, farmers plowed the land and sowed seed. The crop had to be harvested before the next flood.

In October, the flood water began to withdraw, leaving behind on the fields a layer of black and fertile mud.

Between October and June, the Nile flowed within its banks.

MAKING AN OASIS

DISTRIBUTING THE WATER
Water arriving in the palm grove is distributed by comb-like devices, which regulate the flow and divert the water into a large number of secondary channels. The larger the gaps between the "teeth" of the comb, the greater the volume of water allowed through to the gardens of individual landowners.

An oasis is not a naturally-occurring island of vegetation around a spring in the desert; it is very much a human creation. People living in the desert have learned to exploit aquifers – places underground where water gathers, often as a result of rain falling far away. Many oases are located at the meeting point of a network of tunnels, some of them miles in length, which the desert-dwellers have built in order to tap underground pockets of water. The water is first taken to use – very sparingly – for the domestic needs of the village. Then it runs downhill to the oasis, where it is channeled to palm groves and vegetable gardens. Abundantly watered, the palm trees grow dense and luxurious, and so protect the carefully cultivated vegetable crops from the desert wind and sun.

The village is fortified and stands just outside the oasis. It is built at a place from which it can control and defend access to the water supply. Waste water from the village flows down to irrigate the cultivated land.

WATER CLOCK
Each landowner is allowed to irrigate his garden for a certain length of time. A water clock is used to control this. When his time is up, the owner blocks off his own channel and the water is diverted to the garden of his neighbor.

Water filters down through the sand and may take centuries to reach the oasis.

Underground rock strata (layers) hold rainwater which may have fallen over vast areas of desert, up to hundreds of miles away.

The tunnels and ventilation shafts are wide enough to allow a person access for maintenance work.

The Arabic word qanat *is used for the tunnels built to channel the underground water supplies.*

WATER OWNERSHIP
Each family by the oasis owns a share of the water supply, which is handed down from generation to generation, along with the house and garden. The numbers of "combs" for distributing the water reveal how properties used to be subdivided.

THE ECOSYSTEM OF A PALM GROVE
A palm grove has three levels. The palm fronds (top) protect the fruit trees (middle) from the sun, and these protect the vegetable gardens (bottom). In this way, a relatively humid microclimate is created.

FOSSIL LAKES AND RIVERS
Oases are often formed on the edges of depressions – ancient lake and river beds into which water flows from underground strata, due to gravity.

SPRINGS

From ancient times, springs were worshiped for their life-giving properties. Their clear, pure waters bubbling up from the ground have been a source of curiosity, explained in various ways. For example, some people said that springs were fed by the rivers of the underworld; some, that spring water mysteriously percolated up from the ocean depths; and others, that they were the result of water vapor condensing in icy caverns deep inside the Earth. Not until the eighteenth century, when geology and underground rock formations were better understood, did the cause of springs become clear. Rainwater filters down through permeable layers of sand and loose materials until it is blocked by impermeable layers of clay or compact rock. Here it accumulates and flows over the surface, finally emerging into the light of day after a long journey underground.

MINERAL WATER
At the end of the nineteenth century, fear of catching typhoid fever from contaminated water supplies led people to drink bottled spring water. Since then, particularly recently, bottled water has become widely popular.

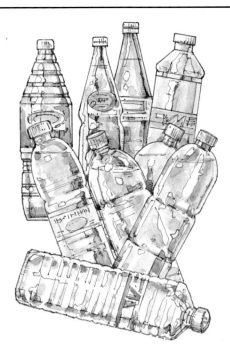

PLASTIC
The first plastic bottle for mineral water was produced in France in 1968.

AQUIFERS
Water filters down through permeable rock and sometimes collects in a layer called an aquifer. Aquifers feed springs. The water in an aquifer can also be tapped by digging a well.

Permeable layers.

Impermeable clay.

Well.

Aquifer.

Spring.

Stream.

KARST REGIONS

In limestone areas, instead of forming rivers, rainwater filters down through the rock, dissolving the calcium carbonate and gradually carving out potholes and underground passages. Eventually underground rivers form, which may re-emerge as springs.

ANTONIO VALLISNIERI
(1661-1730)
In 1726, this Italian doctor and naturalist put an end to questions about the origin of springs. Following a series of close investigations, he showed that springs depended on rainfall.

THERMAL SPRINGS

The therapeutic properties of warm springs rich in mineral salts have been known since ancient times. Going to "take the waters," for one's health, later became a popular practice, giving people a reason to undertake foreign travel. Fashionable cities grew up around thermal baths.

"Fountain of Life," a fifteenth-century illustration.

"The Virtues of Bathing," thirteenth century.

ANCIENT MYTHS

In ancient Greece, springs were treated as sacred. They were thought to be the homes of nymphs, each with its own special myth.

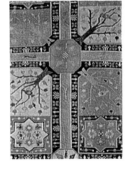

THE RIVERS OF PARADISE

This antique Persian carpet represents the Garden of Eden. Its Arab makers took up the ancient Biblical tradition that the sources of four of the world's great rivers – the Nile, the Tigris, the Euphrates and the Indus – were found in the Garden.

THIRSTY CITIES

ANCIENT ROME

Rome's system of aqueducts (shown in red on the map above) was built between the fourth century BC and the second century AD. The overground parts, whose magnificent ruins are so admired today, were in fact only the "tip of the iceberg": 29 miles (47 km) of aqueduct ran overground, but the greater part of the system consisted of a network of more than 235 miles (380 km) of underground channels. These collected water from the springs and mountain streams of the surrounding area.

Cities were nearly always built near springs or by the side of rivers and lakes, whose water they could use. However, as they grew, it became necessary also to import water from more distant sources. The ancient Romans built great aqueducts, the impressive ruins of which can still be seen in many countries. These aqueducts brought water to large urban populations, whose needs could not have been met by local wells and springs. In imperial times, Rome had roughly one million inhabitants and was served by no fewer than eleven aqueducts. Every day, these carried some 1,170,000 cubic yards (900,000 cu m) of water to the city, or 234 gallons (900 l) per person – double the amount of water available to each inhabitant of Rome today.

MANAGING THE WATER SUPPLY

A special magistrate was responsible for managing the water supply of ancient Rome. Under him were an architect, a number of civil servants, and a host of slaves who performed the building and other manual tasks.

Water collected from a spring, often on the site of a temple, was decanted into a two-part reservoir to remove impurities.

Most of the system was underground. The water was channeled in cement pipes with shafts at 164 ft (50 m) intervals to allow for inspection and cleaning.

Frontinus, the magistrate responsible for Rome's water supply at the end of the first century AD, said that 17 percent of the available water was for the emperor. It was piped directly to his palace, where it supplied swimming pools and fountains.

To maintain a constant gradient, or incline, bridges were built across valleys, often with several tiers of arches. The most famous is the Pont du Gard in the south of France.

The optimum gradient was under 2 percent. To maintain this gentle slope, an aqueduct could often not follow the most direct route; hence the curves.

The reservoirs into which the aqueducts discharged were in the upper part of the city, so that the water could be distributed by gravity.

The reservoirs had three main outlets supplying water to public buildings, private dwellings, and the emperor's palace.

Rainwater collected by roof guttering was channeled to a cistern below the main courtyard.

39 percent of the water supply was allocated for domestic use. Private dwellings also had systems for collecting rainwater.

One system of pipes conveyed water to fountains, baths and other public buildings. According to Frontinus, 44 percent of the supply was devoted to such uses. Public fountains alone took 13.5 percent.

27

Water power

The ancient Greeks and Romans knew how to use the force of a river or waterfall to turn a paddle-wheel connected to the grindstone of a mill. However, it was not until the Middle Ages that people realized the enormous potential of this kind of machine. It was soon in use wherever there was a stream or river, first simply for grinding and then, with slight modifications, for sawing timber, making felt, working the bellows of forges and pumping water from mines. From the eleventh century on, water became the most widely used source of energy, and remained so for seven hundred years, until the invention of the steam engine. This was despite competition from the windmill, introduced from the East in the thirteenth century.

Upstream from the dam, the water was diverted from its course to be fed to the mill.

A special gateway was included in the design, to allow tree trunks to pass over the dam.

WINDMILLS
Windmills rivaled the power of water mills. They first appeared in Europe in the thirteenth century and soon became widespread in areas with strong and regular winds. The most common type was the post mill, whose whole body turned on a central wooden post so that the sails could be faced into the wind.

The river was also used for transporting timber.

BUILDING A MILL
For the whole of the Middle Ages, building a water mill also meant major engineering work such as constructing dams and water channels. Such an expensive undertaking could be afforded only by rich landowners or monasteries. Ordinary people were charged for use of a mill, depending on the amount of grain they ground.

The dam caused a deep pool of water to form, so that there was always a regular flow on which the mill could depend.

Wooden pile foundations.

28

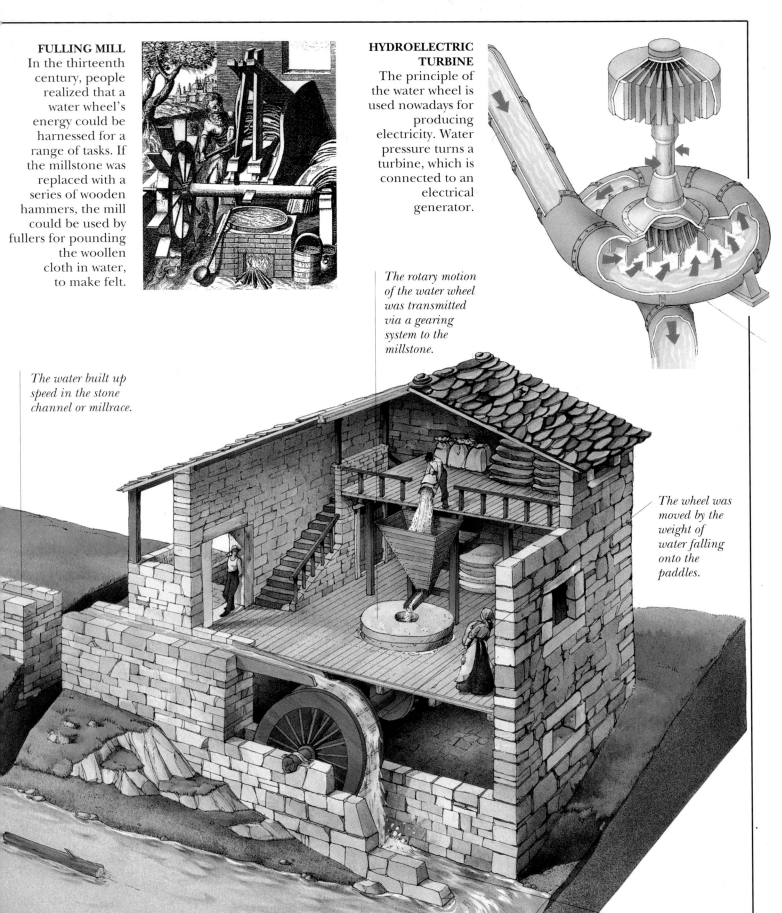

FULLING MILL
In the thirteenth century, people realized that a water wheel's energy could be harnessed for a range of tasks. If the millstone was replaced with a series of wooden hammers, the mill could be used by fullers for pounding the woollen cloth in water, to make felt.

HYDROELECTRIC TURBINE
The principle of the water wheel is used nowadays for producing electricity. Water pressure turns a turbine, which is connected to an electrical generator.

The rotary motion of the water wheel was transmitted via a gearing system to the millstone.

The water built up speed in the stone channel or millrace.

The wheel was moved by the weight of water falling onto the paddles.

Having served its purpose, the water was returned to the main river via the tailrace.

29

RECLAIMING LAND

MALARIA

For centuries, people living in marshy areas fell ill and died from a fever which was thought to be caused by the vapor rising from stagnant water. Both the vapor and the disease were called "malaria," from the Italian words for "bad air." Not until 1880 was it discovered that the disease is caused by a parasite transmitted by the bite of the Anopheles mosquito. Drainage of marshland and use of insecticides have reduced the incidence of the disease in many areas, but malaria is still a widespread killer.

Water in the landscape has its disadvantages. For example, salt marshes at the mouth of rivers and stretches of stagnant water further inland are unhealthy and unsuitable environments for human habitation and agriculture. Through history, marshy land has been reclaimed for human use. It was a difficult task, requiring large numbers of workers and significant investment, as well as a good knowledge of hydraulic engineering. Using slave labor, the ancient Romans reclaimed vast areas of land, but the gains they made were often short-lived. In the Middle Ages, the Dutch were more successful: they developed highly sophisticated techniques for winning land from the sea, and so were able to reclaim permanently the flood-plains at the mouths of the Rhine and Meuse rivers. Beginning in the seventeenth century, many nations drew on the Dutch experience to reclaim land and make it productive.

Land periodically flooded by the sea could be reclaimed.

It was surrounded by dikes, to protect it from the sea at high tide.

Two channels at right angles to each other encouraged water to drain away as the tide was going out.

THE DUTCH POLDERS

To drain areas of low-lying land at the mouths of rivers, the Dutch began by building dikes to stop water flowing in at high tide. The land enclosed by the dikes was then drained by letting the water flow away as the tide was going out.

The sea tends to deposit sand along the coast, forming dunes. This stops rivers discharging directly into the sea, and marshland develops.

Draining coastal marshland gives large areas of fertile alluvial soil suitable for agriculture.

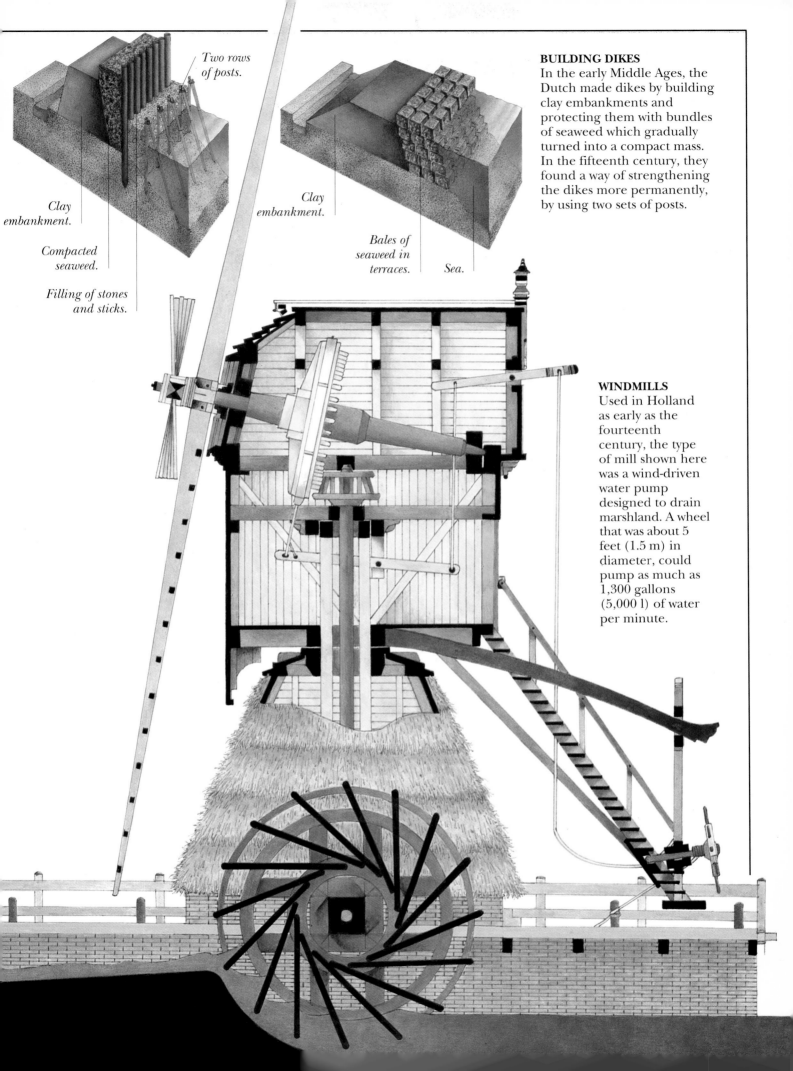

Two rows of posts.

Clay embankment.

Compacted seaweed.

Filling of stones and sticks.

Clay embankment.

Bales of seaweed in terraces.

Sea.

BUILDING DIKES

In the early Middle Ages, the Dutch made dikes by building clay embankments and protecting them with bundles of seaweed which gradually turned into a compact mass. In the fifteenth century, they found a way of strengthening the dikes more permanently, by using two sets of posts.

WINDMILLS

Used in Holland as early as the fourteenth century, the type of mill shown here was a wind-driven water pump designed to drain marshland. A wheel that was about 5 feet (1.5 m) in diameter, could pump as much as 1,300 gallons (5,000 l) of water per minute.

CANALS

Rivers, especially those with a regular flow, have always been an important means of transportation. River transport is suitable in particular for bulky goods, such as grain, wine, coal, timber and sand, and has the advantage of being cheaper than transport by road. But not all rivers are navigable, and even navigable rivers do not always lead in the right direction! Where this was the case, the answer was to dig canals linking rivers to centers of trade and industry. Canal building began in the twelfth century and by the seventeenth century much of central Europe was served by a dense canal network. The invention of the lock made it possible for vessels to move between bodies of water at different heights. A spectacular example of canal engineering is the 155 mile (250 km) Canal du Midi, in the south of France. Connecting the Atlantic with the Mediterranean, it has one hundred locks and is 1,312 feet (400 m) metres above sea level at its highest point.

COMPARING LOADS
A donkey can carry a burden of 22 pounds (100 g) on its back. A horse pulling a cart can move 2,210 pounds (1,000 g). However, the same horse pulling a canal barge can move 132,600 pounds (60,000 kg)!

A canal bridge, enabling vessels to pass over a river.

On reaching a town, the canal widens out to form a port where goods can be loaded and unloaded.

A barge on its way down: the lower lock gate is opened and the water drains out.

A MODERN LOCK
Modern locks are much larger than past examples and can accommodate whole convoys of barges. The opening and closing of the gates are controlled electronically rather than by hand, but the basic principle remains the same.

PIERRE-PAUL RIQUET
(1604-1680)
The building of the Canal du Midi was undertaken by Pierre-Paul Riquet, an adventurous entrepreneur who financed part of the work himself, in return for the right to manage the canal and collect tolls. The building took only twenty years and the canal opened in 1681. But Riquet had died, worn out by his labors, a year before.

The waters feeding the canal must join it at its highest point. Otherwise the water level would drop every time the lock gates were opened.

A lockkeeper's cottage. Traditionally the lockkeeper worked the gates whenever a vessel wanted to pass through.

Rows of trees along the canal help to stabilize the banks.

The sides of the lock are curved. This increases its capacity, as the shape of the lock matches the shape of barges.

A towpath along each bank was for the horses pulling the barges.

In lowland areas, the canal runs between embankments.

THE AGE OF STEAM

At the beginning of the eighteenth century, water was still the most important source of power and therefore no factory could be built far from a stream or river. Industrial premises were crowded into narrow valleys, since ever higher falls of water were needed to drive more and more powerful water wheels and machinery. In fact, raising water was the first task performed by steam engines: they were developed in Britain to pump water from coal mines. These machines might have remained no more than a clever form of pump if it had not been for the Scottish engineer, James Watt. In 1781 he invented a way of converting the up-and-down piston movement of a steam engine into rotary motion. This enabled the steam engine to become a new source of power, giving life to the Industrial Revolution. Steam engines, which needed only relatively small quantities of water, were more powerful than any water-driven machinery, and another great advantage was that they could be installed anywhere.

INDUSTRIAL TOWNS
At the end of the eighteenth century, industrial towns became full of workshops and factories, where men, women and children labored for more than ten hours per day.

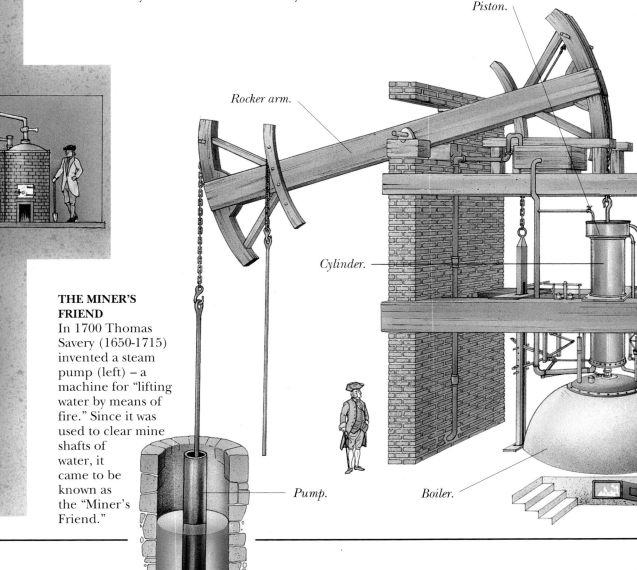

Piston.

Rocker arm.

Cylinder.

THE MINER'S FRIEND
In 1700 Thomas Savery (1650-1715) invented a steam pump (left) – a machine for "lifting water by means of fire." Since it was used to clear mine shafts of water, it came to be known as the "Miner's Friend."

Pump.

Boiler.

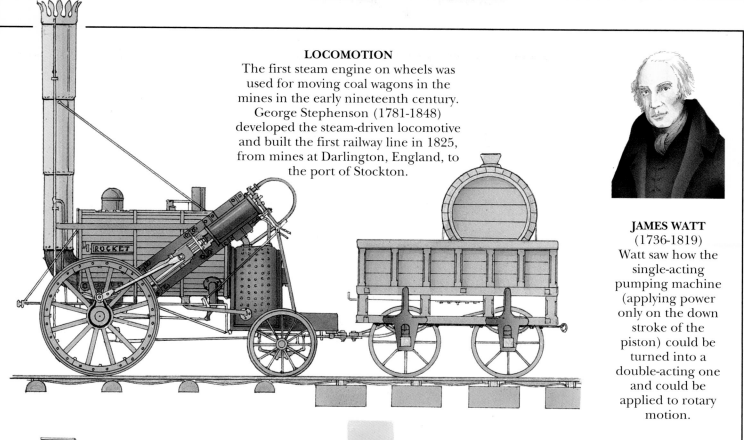

LOCOMOTION

The first steam engine on wheels was used for moving coal wagons in the mines in the early nineteenth century. George Stephenson (1781-1848) developed the steam-driven locomotive and built the first railway line in 1825, from mines at Darlington, England, to the port of Stockton.

JAMES WATT

(1736-1819) Watt saw how the single-acting pumping machine (applying power only on the down stroke of the piston) could be turned into a double-acting one and could be applied to rotary motion.

THE FIRST STEAM ENGINE

Designed for pumping water from mines, the first steam engine was put into service in 1712. It was soon taken up by the Dutch, who used it for draining land. The engine on the left was patented in Britain by Thomas Savery and Thomas Newcomen (1663-1729). Steam from the boiler entered the cylinder and the piston moved up. The plunger of the pump moved down. Cooling water was then added. Air pressure in the mine forced the piston down and this lifted the plunger.

WATT'S STEAM ENGINE

In Watt's rotating engine, the end of the rocker arm was connected to a rod which turned a shaft. This arrangement converted the up-and-down motion of the piston into circular motion, making possible many new applications. Watt's steam engine was used in particular in the textile industry, to power both looms and spinning machinery.

IMPROVEMENTS IN HYGIENE

THE WATER CARRIER
The public water carrier was still a familiar figure in towns at the beginning of the nineteenth century. Water came mainly from wells. The few piped water systems that did exist supplied public pumps and, at the very most, the lower floors of better-off private houses.

LOUIS PASTEUR
(1822-1895)
In 1857, the French chemist and microbiologist Louis Pasteur announced his discovery that the fermentation of alcohol and of milk was caused by microorganisms. Later he showed that microorganisms were also the cause of disease. He demonstrated that disease spreads rapidly in unclean conditions where the microorganisms (bacteria) thrive.

In the early nineteenth century, hygiene was rudimentary – and this was most obvious in rapidly-growing cities such as London and Paris. In the poorer areas, water was generally supplied only to public pumps and even in middle-class houses water was piped only to ground-floor level. New water-supply systems improved conditions for the growing city populations, and yet water quality was not well monitored and epidemics of typhoid and cholera, caused by polluted water, were still frequent. Drains were antiquated and not really intended to carry away anything other than rain water. Very few houses had toilets. Most waste ended up in cesspools, whose contents were collected at regular intervals to be used as manure for market gardens. It was not until the second half of the century that sewage systems were modernized and flushing toilets replaced toilets that emptied into cesspools. Even then, there was resistance from the companies which had previously made big profits from the collection of waste.

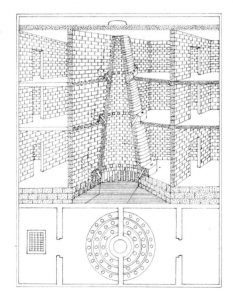

COMMUNAL TOILETS
Toilets designed in 1786 for the Salpêtrière hospital in Paris were arranged around a tall, ventilated cone-shaped structure. Waste fell down inside the cone to the main sewer.

New, closed-in sewers were built, following the same routes as the old open sewers and depending on the slope of the land.

In the past, most cities simply discharged their sewage into natural drainage channels such as streams and ditches. Eventually, closed-in sewer systems were built.

CONVENIENT SEATS

Before the invention of toilets, some people had "close stools" or commodes. These consisted of a chamber pot hidden inside a seat which was often luxuriously padded. The seat shown on the right was a development of this. It contained a bucket which would be filled with sand to deal with smells.

THE TOILET

In the 1590s Sir John Harington invented a flushing toilet for Queen Elizabeth I. But this was a unique early example. It was only from the end of the eighteenth century that manufacturers like Doulton developed toilets, with a U-bend and flush mechanism. From then, they became widespread.

VACUUM (PATENT)

DOULTON & Co
SANITARY ENGINEERS
LONDON & PAISLEY

CLEAN HANDS

In 1848, Ignaz Semmelweiss, a doctor of Hungarian origin, found the cause of a fever that killed many mothers who gave birth in hospital. It was that doctors and medical students caring for the women were not washing their hands after dissecting dead bodies.

MANURE

Some people made a lot of money by removing and selling organic refuse, particularly excrement, as manure. In the late nineteenth century, specialized companies employed workers to collect the contents of cesspools every night.

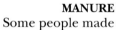

HAVING A BATH

From medieval times until the eighteenth century, people rarely washed. In fact, many doctors claimed that washing was bad for health. At Louis XIV's court at Versailles, water was channeled in abundance to monumental fountains, but baths did not exist. When people did bathe, it was in portable bathtubs that were filled with hot water – sometimes for use by several people in turn.

WATER SUPPLY AND SEWAGE

The water-supply system of a modern city is designed to deliver 130 gallons (500 l) per person per day. This means that a city of one million people needs 130,000,000 gallons (500,000,000 l) of water every day. It is pumped from wells, rivers and other sources which are often quite far away. It is treated to make it fit for human consumption, and then introduced, under pressure, into the distribution network. After use, the waste water runs away into drains, which convey it by gravity to a specially designed purification plant. The two networks – water supply and sewage disposal – in fact constitute a single system. Generally, the volume of clean water distributed is greater than the volume actually used, because there are leaks in every water-supply system. Sometimes up to 30 percent of the water supply is wasted.

WATER TREATMENT

In a treatment plant, water is purified to make it safe for drinking. Impurities are removed and germs destroyed by processes of sedimentation and filtering, and by the addition of chlorine.

The height of the reservoir gives the pressure necessary for the water to be distributed.

Sulphur dioxide is added to eliminate chlorine.

Filtration and sterilization plant.

Basin collecting waste from the sedimentation process.

The water is distributed from the reservoir to buildings in the city.

In the sedimentation tank, chlorine and slaked lime are added.

Water is pumped from a river.

LONDON
At the beginning of the nineteenth century, huge machines pumped water from the Thames to supply London. The river's water level fell so much that shipping was affected.

Water reaches the upper floors of buildings because it is under pressure in the pipes.

Every tap supplying water is matched by a waste pipe conveying used water to the drains.

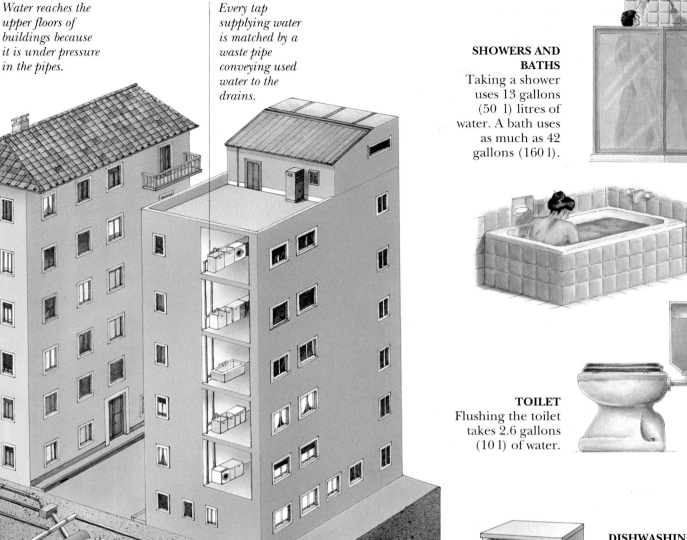

Sewers are oval in cross-section, an efficient shape for carrying away waste matter.

Tank for sedimentation of solid waste.

Plant for separating sewage and sludge.

Tank for treating sludge.

Filtered and purified, the water is discharged back into the river.

SHOWERS AND BATHS
Taking a shower uses 13 gallons (50 l) litres of water. A bath uses as much as 42 gallons (160 l).

TOILET
Flushing the toilet takes 2.6 gallons (10 l) of water.

DISHWASHING
A dishwasher uses 21 gallons (80 l) of water; doing the same amount of dishwashing by hand takes about 10 gallons (40 l).

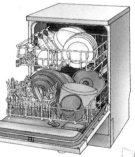

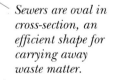

SEWAGE TREATMENT
The treatment of raw sewage involves various stages of sedimentation, to allow suspended solids to settle, and a stage of aeration. During aeration, organic pollutants are "digested" by microorganisms. They form what is called "activated sludge."

DOMESTIC CONSUMPTION
A person needs only 2 or 3 quarts of drinking water per day, and could get by on about 20 for washing and cooking purposes. However, daily consumption in a modern household tends to be much greater, as shown above.

POLLUTION

As we have seen, the world's water is constantly being recycled through the natural processes of evaporation, precipitation and runoff. It is also naturally purified by the biological activity of aquatic organisms which digest organic wastes. However, it has become increasingly difficult for the Earth's water supplies to keep purifying themselves in this way. Nature now has to cope with new chemical compounds which will not break down, such as plastics; many different kinds of chemical wastes produced by industrial processes; and concentrations of sewage from growing cities. These kinds of pollution have led to the destruction of life in lakes and rivers. A less visible but very serious result of the pollution is that an increasing percentage of the world's limited water supply is being rendered unfit for human use.

INDUSTRIAL WASTE
It is possible that some of the chemical wastes that are released into rivers by modern industry may poison the water.

URBAN WASTE
If too much sewage is discharged into a river, the organisms in the water may be unable to break down the waste matter.

RIVERS
Organic waste dumped in rivers is broken down by bacteria in the water. This process uses oxygen. If too much waste is dumped, the oxygen in the water may be used up before the river has purified itself. Fish thrive in water that is rich in organic matter, but without enough oxygen they very soon die.

When water used to cool a nuclear reactor is returned to a river, it raises its temperature. This causes changes in plant and animal life.

Industrial waste.

Urban waste.

ACID RAIN
Industries and vehicle exhausts give off gases (including sulphur dioxide and nitrogen oxides) which combine with water vapor in the air, forming acid rain. This rain, which is dilute sulphuric acid, is fatal to vegetation and has led to the destruction of much European woodland.

Acid rain affects forests.

Pesticides sprayed from the air are dangerous to humans and other animals.

Pesticides and fertilizers used in agriculture filter down through the soil and may eventually poison aquifers and the springs that these feed.

ENOUGH WATER TO GO ROUND?

Although it is continually recycled, the Earth's supply of water is limited. Only one fifth of the water that falls on the Earth is actually available for human use. The remainder runs off during torrential rain or falls in uninhabited areas. Furthermore, the water that is available is very unevenly distributed among the different climatic regions of the world. There are a number of human factors which further reduce the amount of water available to us. First, a significant quantity is wasted, either through irresponsible use or as a result of leakages. Second, pollution has made some water supplies unfit for human use, causing disease and death in many parts of the world. Most of all, the rapid growth in world population is a threat to water supplies. By the year 2000, world demand for water will be five times greater than in 1940: every time the population doubles, the water available per inhabitant is halved.

AVAILABILITY
The amount of water available per person varies from over 130,000 cubic yards (100,000 cu m) per year (in Canada) to less than 1,300 (1,000 cu m) in arid countries. According to a United Nations estimate, in 1990 31 percent of the people in developing countries did not have access to clean water; 46 percent lacked proper sewage systems.

WATER CONSUMPTION
26 gallons (100 l) of water are used to produce 2.2 lb (1 kg) of steel; 208 gallons (800 l) for 2.21 lb (1 kg) of wheat; and 7,800 gallons (30,000 l) for 2.2 lb (1 kg) of beef! This is taking into account the water needed to grow fodder for the bull.

THE ARAL SEA
Once the world's third largest lake, the Aral Sea now ranks only sixth. This is because the rivers that once replenished it have been diverted for irrigation purposes. Two thirds of the lake water – 143 cubic miles (600 cu km) – have already been taken.

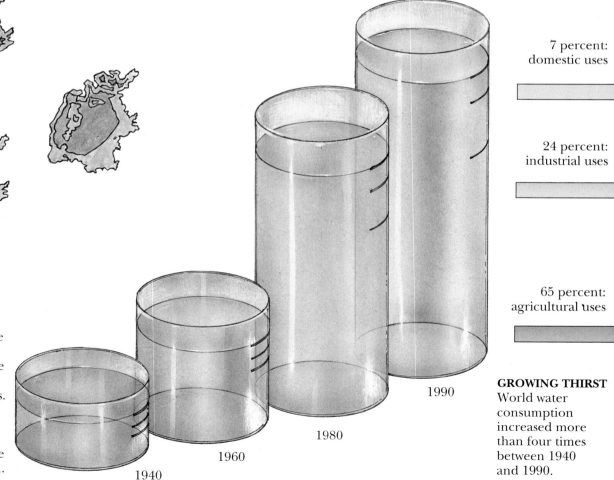

1940

1960

1980

1990

7 percent: domestic uses

24 percent: industrial uses

65 percent: agricultural uses

GROWING THIRST
World water consumption increased more than four times between 1940 and 1990.

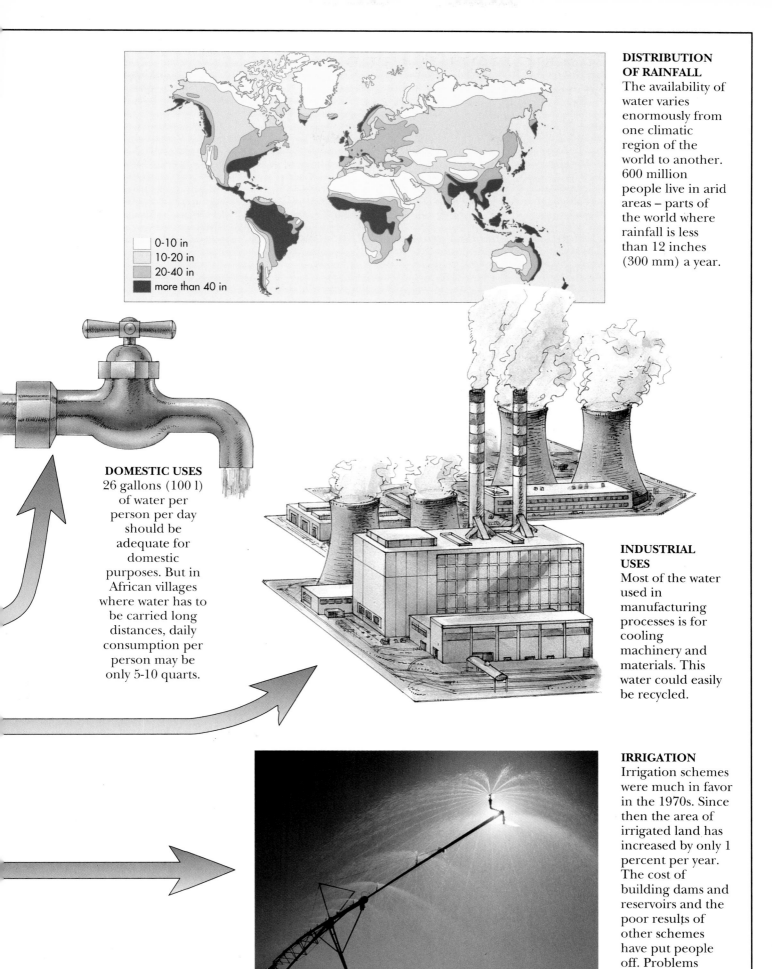

DISTRIBUTION OF RAINFALL
The availability of water varies enormously from one climatic region of the world to another. 600 million people live in arid areas – parts of the world where rainfall is less than 12 inches (300 mm) a year.

0-10 in
10-20 in
20-40 in
more than 40 in

DOMESTIC USES
26 gallons (100 l) of water per person per day should be adequate for domestic purposes. But in African villages where water has to be carried long distances, daily consumption per person may be only 5-10 quarts.

INDUSTRIAL USES
Most of the water used in manufacturing processes is for cooling machinery and materials. This water could easily be recycled.

IRRIGATION
Irrigation schemes were much in favor in the 1970s. Since then the area of irrigated land has increased by only 1 percent per year. The cost of building dams and reservoirs and the poor results of other schemes have put people off. Problems included leakages and salinization of the soil.

THE FUTURE

"Let us not allow a single raindrop to return to the sea without having served humankind." So wrote King Parakrama Bahu of Sri Lanka, way back in the twelfth century. In the future, as the world population continues to grow, the efficient use of water supplies will be a principal concern of all countries. New solutions must be found to cope with shortages and increasing pollution. On the one hand, existing water resources need to be used more efficiently by recycling and conservation. On the other, the amount of fresh water available must be increased. In view of the difficulties involved in pumping up deep-lying groundwater, it is likely that more fresh water will have to be made from the sea. In many countries around the world, especially those with an arid climate, some of these ideas are already being put into practice.

WASTING LESS
Faced with the prospect of serious water shortages, Mexico has introduced a series of reforms to reduce water consumption per person by one sixth before the end of the twentieth century. In particular, toilet tanks are being replaced with smaller models holding about 6 quarts. This measure will soon be saving enough water to meet the needs of 250,000 people.

REDUCING CONSUMPTION
In Europe and the United States, the amount of water used has not increased since the 1970s and, thanks to new conservation measures, should decrease slightly by the end of the century.

DRIP-FEED IRRIGATION
In many cases, only 45 percent of the water used in irrigation actually reaches the plants. The effectiveness of irrigation can be improved considerably by using low-pressure spray systems or by supplying water directly to the roots drop by drop. Computerized control systems are being developed to ensure that plants receive just the amount of water they need.

RECYCLING
For agriculture, it is often feasible to use water of inferior quality, such as water extracted from industrial or urban wastes.

ICEBERGS
The polar icecaps are the world's biggest reservoirs of fresh water. Therefore one idea for boosting water supplies is to tow huge icebergs to arid regions. Even if some of the ice melted on the way, an enormous quantity of fresh water would reach its destination, still locked up in the iceberg. It could then be pumped directly into the ground to replenish exhausted aquifers.

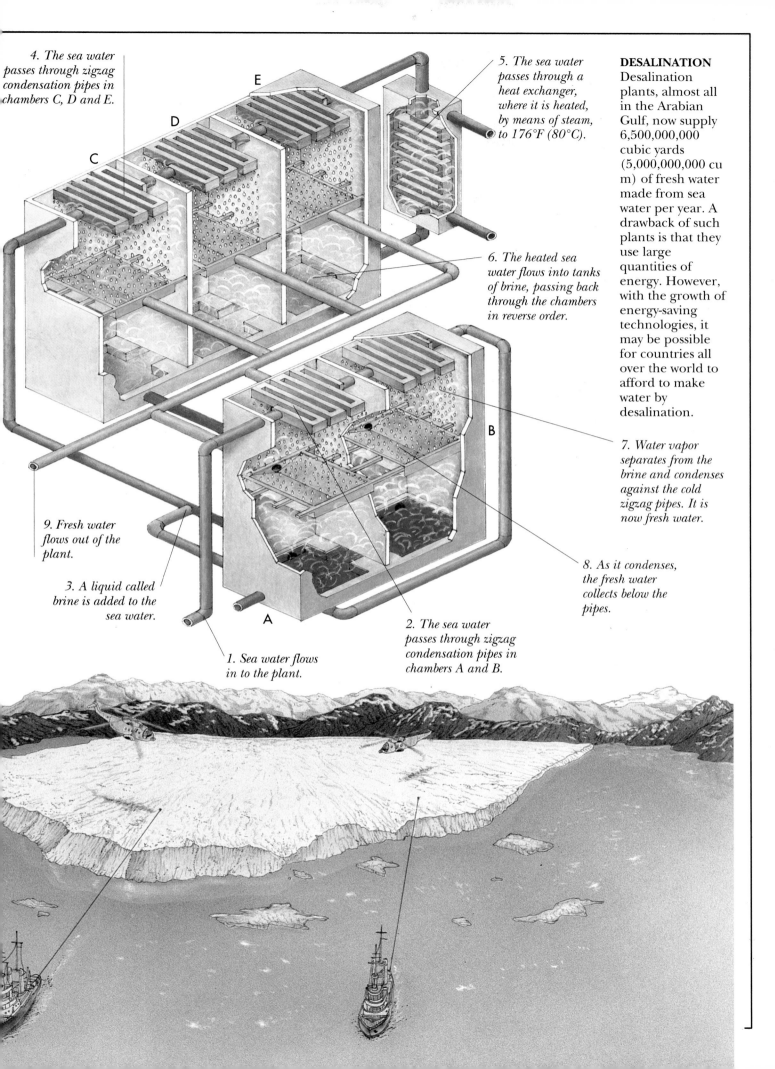

4. The sea water passes through zigzag condensation pipes in chambers C, D and E.

5. The sea water passes through a heat exchanger, where it is heated, by means of steam, to 176°F (80°C).

6. The heated sea water flows into tanks of brine, passing back through the chambers in reverse order.

E

D

C

B

A

DESALINATION
Desalination plants, almost all in the Arabian Gulf, now supply 6,500,000,000 cubic yards (5,000,000,000 cu m) of fresh water made from sea water per year. A drawback of such plants is that they use large quantities of energy. However, with the growth of energy-saving technologies, it may be possible for countries all over the world to afford to make water by desalination.

7. Water vapor separates from the brine and condenses against the cold zigzag pipes. It is now fresh water.

8. As it condenses, the fresh water collects below the pipes.

9. Fresh water flows out of the plant.

3. A liquid called brine is added to the sea water.

2. The sea water passes through zigzag condensation pipes in chambers A and B.

1. Sea water flows in to the plant.

GLOSSARY

ALLUVIAL SOIL Soil deposited by rivers or floods. It consists of fine grains and is very fertile.

AQUIFER Underground rock layer which collects and holds water. Aquifers may consist of sedimentary and porous volcanic rocks, fractured and cracked rocks, and loose deposits of sand and gravel. (See also WATER-BEARING STRATUM.)

BRINE A liquid used in the process of desalinating sea water. It is also used in refrigeration equipment.

CONDENSATION The process whereby a substance changes from a gaseous to a liquid state. Water vapor condenses to form water when the temperature falls. (See also PRECIPITATION.)

DECANT To let a liquid flow out of a container, without disturbing solid particles in it which have settled at the bottom. The process helps to purify the water.

DELTA The mouth of a river where the water deposits large amounts of material which the sea currents and tides cannot disperse. Sandbanks and islands therefore form. A delta is usually triangular in shape and the river tends to divide into a number of channels.

DESALINATION The process of converting sea water into fresh water by removing its salt content.

DRAINAGE System for ensuring that rainwater runs away and does not form stagnant pools.

DRAINAGE BASIN Area of land in which all water falling as rain or snow runs via ditches, streams or other watercourses into a single river or lake, or into the sea.

ECOSYSTEM Community of organisms which depend on each other for survival and the environment in which they live.

EROSION The action of water or wind wearing away rock. In the case of water, it breaks off fragments of rock on sloping ground, carries them away and eventually breaks them down into smaller pieces.

EVAPOTRANSPIRATION The discharge of water into the atmosphere by both the evaporation of water from the Earth's surface and transpiration – the giving off of water vapor by the leaves of plants.

HYDROELECTRIC DAM Dam on a watercourse, holding back the water and forming an artificial lake. The stored water is used to produce electricity and for irrigating the surrounding fertile land.

HYDROLOGY Study of the origins, distribution and physical and chemical composition of the Earth's water resources.

IMPERMEABLE ROCK Rock which does not allow fluids to seep through it.

IRRIGATED AGRICULTURE Farming which does not rely only on rainfall to water crops, but which supplies water to the plants by one of several types of irrigation systems.

MEANDER Wide curve formed by a river in its lowland stage. Meanders form when the river is forced to make a way around the material it has deposited on its banks.

MESOLITHIC PERIOD Middle Stone Age. Period of human prehistory between the Paleolithic (Old Stone Age) and Neolithic (New Stone Age) periods. It saw the first attempts to domesticate animals.

METEOROLOGY Study of the Earth's atmosphere and the effects that atmospheric changes have on climate and weather.

MICROORGANISM Organism that can be seen only with the aid of a microscope.

NEOLITHIC PERIOD New Stone Age. The most recent period of prehistory, characterized by the making of polished stone, bone and wooden tools, and by early developments in agriculture.

PALEOLITHIC PERIOD Old Stone Age. The first period of early human history, thought to have lasted for at least two million years. During this period, humans learned to make tools of crudely-worked stone.

PERMEABLE ROCK Rock through which fluids can seep.

PRECIPITATION Water reaching the Earth's surface as a result of atmospheric condensation, in the form of rain, snow, mist, etc.

RAINFALL-DEPENDANT AGRICULTURE Type of farming in which crops are watered exclusively by natural rainfall. In semi-arid areas, it goes by the name of "dry farming."

RECLAMATION All the operations involved in draining marshy or water-covered land and converting it to agricultural (or other) use.

RECYCLING The recovery and reuse of discarded and waste products. Water used by industrial plants and sewage can also be recycled.

RUNOFF The process by which water that has fallen on land runs from higher ground to lower and eventually makes its way to the sea.

SALINITY The quantity of salt contained in a given amount of a substance such as water or soil.

SEDIMENTARY ROCK Rock formed when sand and other particles have accumulated by sedimentation on the bed of a sea or river and have later consolidated when exposed to the atmosphere.

SEDIMENTATION Natural phenomenon whereby a river, as it reaches lower ground and its speed lessens, deposits the small particles (of sand, mud, etc.) it was carrying.

SEWAGE Waste matter that passes through sewers.

WATER-BEARING STRATUM Layer of permeable rock or material immediately above an impermeable one. It tends to collect water filtering down from the surface.

WATER PURIFICATION The various physical and chemical processes used to remove pollutants from water and make it fit for human consumption.

WATERSHED In mountainous areas, the ridge or crest line separating two drainage basins. Rain falling on either side of the watershed will run off towards one river system or the other.

WATER WHEEL Machine driven by running water. It generally takes the form of a vertical paddle wheel, which is made to turn by water falling on it. As the wheel turns, motion is transmitted to a system of gears.

INDEX

Eyewitness
ENERGY

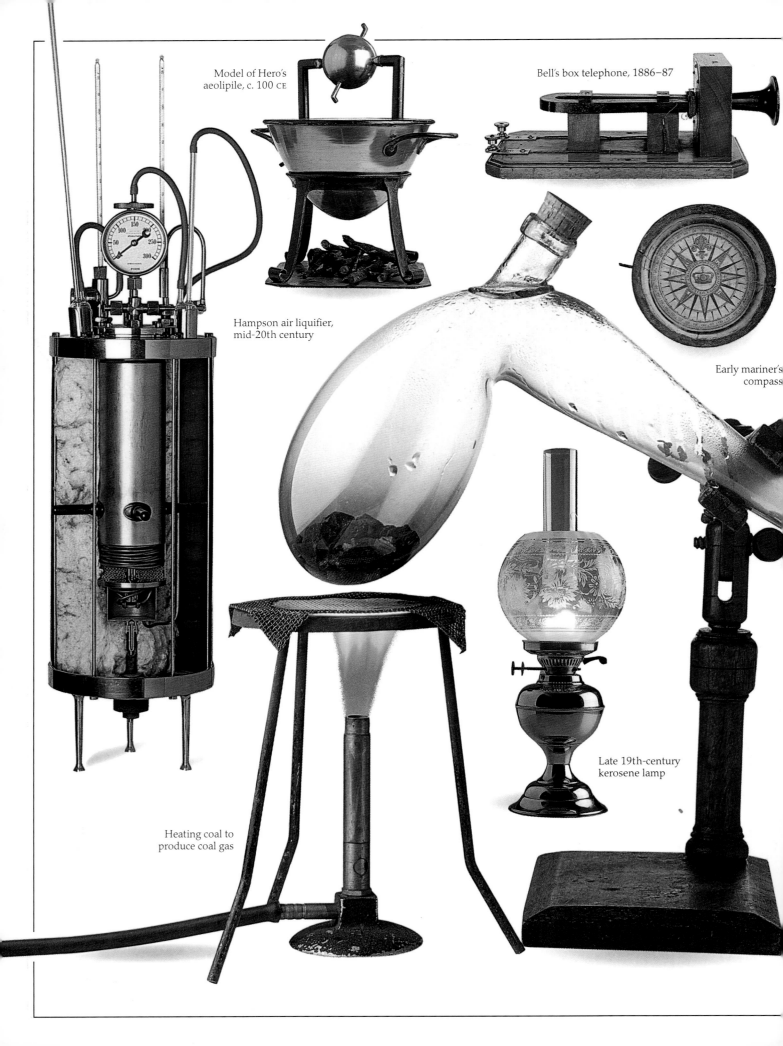

Model of Hero's aeolipile, c. 100 CE

Bell's box telephone, 1886–87

Early mariner's compass

Hampson air liquifier, mid-20th century

Late 19th-century kerosene lamp

Heating coal to produce coal gas